How 24 Year Old Mom Makes $2,000 a Week with a Home Based Business that only costs her $40 to start and $20 per month to operate.

Follow The Author on Twitter
https://twitter.com/jhigginslive

Amazon Related Topics Answered In This Book!

- Work From Home Proof
- Work From Home Jobs
- Work From Home Make Money Online
- Work From Home Businesses
- Work From Home Mom
- Work From Home Free Kindle Books
- Work From Home Free Book
- Work From Home Jobs 101 Real Companies That Pay

Google Related Topics Answered In This Book!

- Work From Home Jobs
- Legitimate Work From Home Jobs
- Legit Work From Home Jobs

Work From Home Opportunities

Top 5 Book On Amazon Related To Working From Home:

1.) http://amzn.to/1cnskPM
2.) http://amzn.to/1d7d23i
3.) http://amzn.to/1bvFZa2
4.) http://amzn.to/1aSYl16
5.) http://amzn.to/1bBkk0Z

Table of Contents

Amazon Related Topics Answered In This Book!

Google Related Topics Answered In This Book!

Top 5 Book On Amazon Related To Working From Home:

Social Proof

The Services Breakdown

Compensation for your Referral

The Benefits Package

Bonus Value

Is it worth it?

6 More Videos

Steps To Get Started

Final Thoughts

Introduction
How I Found Out About Krystal Taylor

It was March 2013 and I *(just like anyone else looking to make additional income online)* was searching the Internet for a real online business. In my research I concluded that there are only 4 really good ways to make a constant income online.

1.) Affiliate Marketing or Network Marketing
2.) Blogging with Google Adsense
3.) Publishing an Ebook on Amazon
4.) Creating Youtube Videos with Google Adsense

So the first thing I did was create a blog. I didn't know the first thing to blog about so I started blogging about how to create a website since I am a web designer. In my research I learned that there was a high demand for landing pages. I incorporated in my blog a landing page generator that was getting lots of views on FB. I noticed that people using my landing page generator were affiliate marketers & network marketers. I also noticed lots of people using my landing page generator were promoting a company called MCA.

I Googled MCA and found some links on YouTube about the company. It looked like the same type of affiliate marketing stuff you always see so I really wasn't moved by all of the hyped-up Youtube videos. I really needed a serious and solid way to make money online.

Then I came across something that really caught my attention. A video of a work from home mom that was very genuine and sincere. Her name is Krystal Taylor and she was showing how she made $20,000 in 9 weeks in the MCA Company. She also mentioned that this opportunity was only $40 to start and $20 per month.

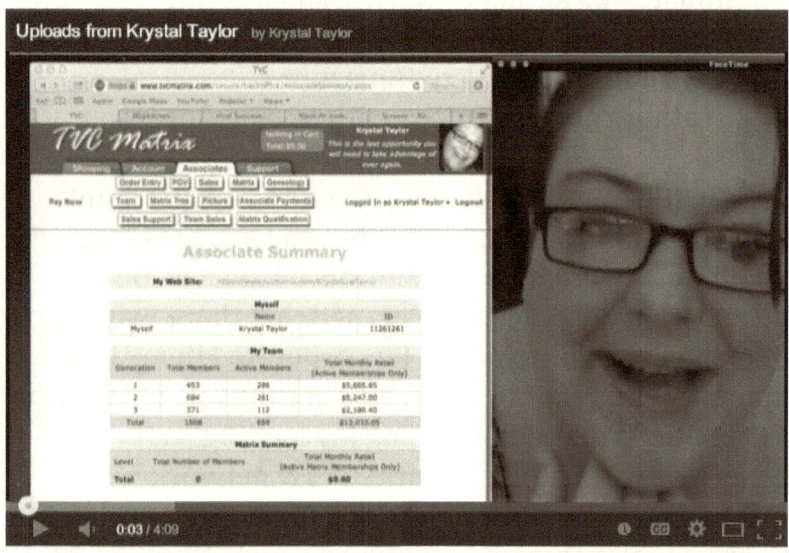

Motor Club Of America - Turn $40 into $2,200 In A Week! Guarant...

This was a reasonable amount for me to invest so I kept watching

She did a complete walkthrough of her back office and pretty much informed everyone that she was not a professional marketer. Me being in Web Design and Marketing felt like if she could do it **so could I.**

Video Link Proof:
https://www.youtube.com/watch?v=lrQNw1iCz6o

Social Proof
Are others having success?

I still needed some social proof so I book marked the YouTube page and started looking further in the MCA company. I researched the company and found out that they have been in business since the 1930's. This made me feel comfortable in that this wasn't just some fly by night business. The companies website even had a phone number for a real customer service rep and the company's headquarters is located in Oklahoma City. I called the customer service line and the service rep answered all of my questions regarding the opportunity. This also indicated that this company was highly profitable. Not many companies can afford services reps and support.

The Services Breakdown
What is the basic flow of this work from home opportunity?

Basically this is how the workflow goes. MCA Stands for Motor Club of America. Their services are comparable to Triple AAA services, which are:

✔ Emergency Roadside Assistance: 24/7 towing up to 100 miles, Tire changing, etc.

✔ Identity Theft Protection: Credit card protection for stolen Credit Card

There are many more services offered. See the below MCA Services Video for full list of MCA Services.

Compensation for your Referral
How much do you make for referring someone to MCA for Emergency Roadside Assistance?

MCA Total Security Motor Club!
100 mile Towing! Legal Benefits!
$50,000 AD&D with Hospital Indemnity and ER Benefit!
$19.95/month. **Get Started!**

When you refer someone to the $19.95 per month service you receive $80 on your next check. The pay period starts every week on Sunday and ends every week on Saturday. Then you receive a check the following Friday for any compensation that you made. You get a back office so you can see your commissions as they come in. You also will receive a benefits card in the mail so you can start having Motor Club coverage. You get motor club coverage and a website to refer others for only $40.00 down & $19.95 per month.

The Benefits Package
What The Benefits Package Looks Like

Bonus Value
How profitable can the MCA opportunity become

Every time you refer someone to the 19.95 per month plan they have an opportunity to receive a free website so they can also send their referrals. You make $6 every time someone you refer makes a referral to their website.

Is it worth it?
My small opportunity evaluation checklist

I began looking further and found more people making money with this company working from home. I did a small checklist to see if this company was worth investing time and energy.

Q.) Was this online opportunity cost effective?

A.) Yes, $40 to start and $20 per month

Q.) Did this online opportunity have legitimate contact information?
A.) Yes, I spoke to a service rep and they answered all of my questions

Q.) Social Proof: Were other people making money with this online opportunity
A.) Yes, I even spoke to other people receiving a real paycheck

Q.) How often did they pay their affiliates?
A.) MCA pays their affiliates every single week via direct deposit or check on a Friday

Meet Steven Rachel
Steven Rachel has retired from the MCA opportunity

This is Steven Rachel. I called Steven to see if his MCA Check was legitimate and found out that not only was his check legitimate but he also moved to Las Vegas, Nevada and retired. This is all that he does now.

6 More Videos

Steve showed me the videos that have the entire company history and breakdown for MCA.

1.) MCA Introduction Video

https://www.youtube.com/watch?v=k-3xJlY0lVg

2.) MCA Company Video
https://www.youtube.com/watch?v=wcrejTTYo84

3.) MCA Services Video
https://www.youtube.com/watch?v=ZI9j0AQX268

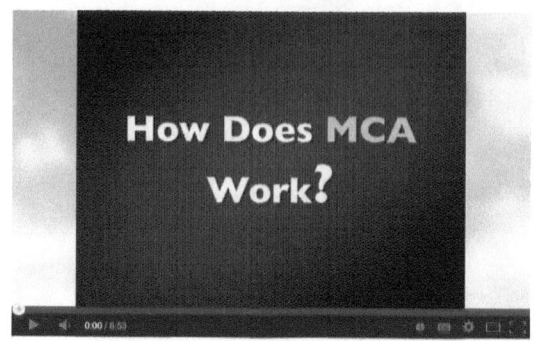

4.) MCA Compensation Video
https://www.youtube.com/watch?v=uhxYxOJMSGg

5.) MCA Marketing Tools Video
https://www.youtube.com/watch?v=vO3nE01dV_8

6.) MCA Training Resources Video
https://www.youtube.com/watch?v=ky0wgXdJMEU

After watching all 6 videos on MCA I was finally convinced that this was a viable and profitable opportunity. "Now how do I sign up?" I was thinking.

If You Are Intrigued by this Opportunity so far please see the rest of the book to find out how to sign up with MCA and start making money.

Steps To Get Started
All I Need is $40 on a debit card or bank card

1.) Go to my website to sign up for the $19.95 per month package. https://www.tvcmatrix.com/jhiggins

If you use my link to sign up I will personally help you with marketing and recruiting through conference calls, coaching and webinars. (Remember I am a web designer, writer, author and marketer. I have some helpful insight.

2.) Call me 707-877-6335 (if I don't pickup then leave message and I'll call you back immediately.) I will walk you through your back office.

3.) Sign-up for an Amazon Affiliate Program. I'm going to show you how to promote your business through Publishing Kindle eBooks and even make more passive income promoting other peoples eBooks.

4.) Follow me on Twitter for my marketing updates and to stay in the loop with important information. https://twitter.com/jhigginslive

Final Thoughts
The reason why I published this eBook

I decided to publish an eBook that can help other people find a legitimate way to make money online because it is just so challenging to find an honest online business. I figure if I can help other people make money then I will have a network of followers that would probably buy my next books, cd's, seminars or workshops. The Law of reciprocity. Give and it will be given unto you!

I sincerely hope you have found this eBook helpful. – J.Higgins

Bonues
More Top Working At Home Books on Amazon Here

1.) Top 5 Affiliate Marketing Books
http://amzn.to/J3i4oC
http://amzn.to/1e402kc
http://amzn.to/J3idbp
http://amzn.to/1e408IC
http://amzn.to/18STTFz

2.) Top 5 Blogging with Google Adsense
http://amzn.to/1bvHSDA
http://amzn.to/1d7e4wc
http://amzn.to/1e40hfg
http://amzn.to/1bBnEcu

http://amzn.to/18AUyJ8

3.) Top 5 Publishing an Ebook on Amazon
http://amzn.to/1aT1jCR
http://amzn.to/1d7ebYK
http://amzn.to/1e40AGE
http://amzn.to/18AV222
http://amzn.to/1jKy2lH

4.) Top 5 Creating YouTube Videos with Google Adsense
http://amzn.to/18AVzAS
http://amzn.to/1d7enqZ
http://amzn.to/1d7etii
http://amzn.to/1gXykTY
http://amzn.to/1aT2ceB

My Other Books
Please Be Sure To Pick Up my Most Recent Book on Amazon about Bitcoin Mining.
http://amzn.to/18p1YMu

Free Chapter
Free Chapter of my Latest Book

THE 21 DAY BITCOIN BILLIONAIRE

Right Now at the time of writing this book (Dec 2013) a Bitcoin is currently worth a little over $1,000

Dollars. So technically if you owned a million Bitcoins you would be a Bitcoin Billionaire. Here's a little mind exercise to help you start thinking like a Bitcoin Billionaire.

Lets start this mind exercise with a simple Question:

If you started with 1 Bitcoin and doubled your Bitcoin worth every day, how many days would it take for you to become a Bitcoin Billionaire (If the Bitcoin Price stayed above $1000 dollars)?

ANSWER 21 DAYS:

Day 1 - You Have 1 Bitcoin = $1,000 Dollars
Day 2 - 2 Bitcoins = $2,000 Dollars
Day 3 - 4 Bitcoins = $4,000 Dollars
Day 4 - 8 Bitcoins = $8,000 Dollars
Day 5 - 16 Bitcoins = $16,000 Dollars
Day 6 - 32 Bitcoins = $32,000 Dollars
Day 7 - 64 Bitcoins = $64,000 Dollars
Day 8 - 128 Bitcoins = $128,000 Dollars
Day 9 - 256 Bitcoins = $256,000 Dollars
Day 10 - 512 Bitcoins = $512,000 Dollars
Day 11 - 1,024 Bitcoins = 1,024,000 Dollars a.k.a. Millionaire Status
Day 12 - 2,048 Bitcoins = $2,048,000 Dollars
Day 13 - 4,096 Bitcoins = $4,096,000 Dollars
Day 14 - 8,192 Bitcoins = $8,192,000 Dollars
Day 15 - 16,384 Bitcoins = $16,384,000 Dollars
Day 16 - 32,768 Bitcoins = $32,768,000 Dollars

Day 17 - 65,536 Bitcoins = $65,536,000 Dollars
Day 18 - 131,072 Bitcoins = $131,072,000 Dollars
Day 19 - 262,144 Bitcoins = $262,144,000 Dollars
Day 20 - 524,288 Bitcoins = $524,288,000 Dollars
Day 21 - 1,048,577 Bitcoins = 1.04 Billion Dollars a.k.a.
Bitcoin Billionaire

The Bitcoin Phenomenon: The Big Break!

In 2009 Kristoffer Koch of Norway spent $27 Dollars or (150 Kroner) for 5,000 Bitcoins. 4 years later his Bitcoin worth became close to 1 Million Dollars. He exchanged 1/5th of his Bitcoins for actual Norwegian currency and bought an apartment in Toyen, which is considered to be the Norwegian Beverly Hills. Don't believe me just Google It!

Stories like this have been plastered all over the internet by everyone from Bloggers to respected media outlets like Forbes Magazine, The BBC and CNN which gave tremendous credibility to Bitcoin. You can probably guess what happens when a respected media outlet publicizes someone who became rich through some smart Internet investment strategy... As many people as possible suddenly start flocking to it like the Gold Rush of '49.... Thus creating The 2013 Bitcoin Phenomenon!

Remember the Winklevoss Twins who sued Facebook for stealing their idea and popularized by the movie "Social Network"? Well they started a Bitcoin Trust fund and currently own 120,000 Bitcoins turning 11 Million Dollars in investments into 120 Million Dollars!

The Bitcoin Revolution is Looking A lot like the PC Revolution and we don't know how long this will last but we do know 1 thing. People like Kristoffer Koch are really cashing in and changing their lives because of it.

Bit-Tip: Check out this Forbes article on the Winklevosses and Bitcoin's 400 Billion dollar future evaluation:

http://www.forbes.com/sites/afontevecchia/2013/11/12/winklevoss-twins-say-bitcoin-market-to-hit-400b-urge-regulators-not-to-push-innovation-to-china/

LESSON 1:

THE BITCOIN DIFFICULTY & THE MINER MINDSET

"LEARNING BITCOIN"

First 7-Hours "Bit-Ready, Bit-Set, GO!"

Thank you for your purchase. If you enjoyed the read please leave me a rating!
Work From Home Moms & Dads SS Guide

Super Bonus for Work From Home
**Here's even more Work From Home Resources.
Hope I get an awesome rating**

Earlier I Mentioned That There Are 4 Surefire ways to make legitimate money online. Below I will outline my Top 2 with examples for each one.

#1.) Affiliate Marketing
The top Affiliate Marketing Programs are:

Clickbank – They make over $200 Million every year, they have been in operation since 1998 and they have paid out over 2 Billion in revenue. To get started just click the link below and sigup for a Free account:
http://goo.gl/2rEqYf

Top 5 Books on becoming a successful ClickBank Affiliate
http://amzn.to/1e408IC
http://amzn.to/JiNJmz
http://amzn.to/1bZhIvA
http://amzn.to/1j0hSqB
http://amzn.to/1h3qOae

Amazon Associates – This is the #1 affiliate program on the Internet. They make over 50 Billion every year and have paid over 10 Billion to their Affiliates. To get started as an Amazon Affiliate click here:
http://goo.gl/aZ4b1x

Top 5 Books on becoming a successful Amazon Associate
http://amzn.to/1h3ttR8
http://amzn.to/1jT44My
http://amzn.to/1bZkfGn
http://amzn.to/1bZkl0A

http://amzn.to/18o62BS

2.) Blogging with Google Adsense – Google Adsense is the #1 Advertising program on the Internet with over 8 Billion dollars in payouts **Every Year!** To get started Go to www.Google.com/Adsense

Top 5 Books on being successful will Google Adsense
http://amzn.to/1dtPje8
http://amzn.to/1bHOQ9w
http://amzn.to/Jb6fwE
http://amzn.to/Jb6szJ - This guy is a Google Genius
http://amzn.to/1j0ljNQ

One Last Bonus from A-G
Here are the Guru Top 2 Guru Programs for making money with Amazon & Google Adsense

If you want to really become and expert with the #1 & #2 top paying online opportunities take a look at these expert guru programs. I already searched out and found the top selling programs on the Internet.

#1 Making Money with Amazon (only $27)
The awesome thing about this Guru program is that it comes with an Amazon Wordpress theme and 2 Amazon eBooks that give you tons of tips to becoming successful with Amazon Affiliate programs.
http://goo.gl/DUKV21

#2 Making Money with Google Adsense

This program is one of the most highly promoted Google Adsense Guru programs and comes with a 7 Day Free trial.
http://goo.gl/6L359K

Added Bonus: This program also introduces you to making money with Clickbank.

Thank you for your purchase. If you enjoyed the read please leave me a rating!

Work From Home Moms & Dads SS Guide

http://amzn.to/1bHVaOh

www.ingramcontent.com/pod-product-compliance
Lightning Source LLC
Chambersburg PA
CBHW021451170526
45164CB00001B/467